Mark
ord
x
hildren

Mark
Ford
Soft Sift

Du...
Grünbein
Ashes for
Breakfast
Selected Poems
Translated by Michael Hofmann

...Hamilton
Collected
Poems
Edited by Alan Jenkins

KT-475-621

gust
einzahler
e Hotel
heira

Nick
Laird
Go
Giants

Lachlan
Mackinnon
The Jupiter
Collisions

Lachlan
Mackinnon
Small
Hours

dwin
Muir
elected
oems

Bernard
O'Donoghue
Farmers
Cross

Bernard
O'Donoghue
Selected
Poems

Tom
Paulin
Love's
Bonfire

ephen
pender
ew
ollected
oems

Wallace
Stevens
Selected
Poems

Jack
Underwood
Happiness

Adam
Zagajewski
Selected
Poems

To Richard

OCT 2016

This diary belongs to

RICHARD
....

A record of your
first full year as a
man of leisure!

Best wishes

Chris

First published in 2016
by Faber & Faber
Bloomsbury House
74–77 Great Russell Street
London WC1B 3DA

Designed and typeset by Faber & Faber Ltd
Printed in China by Imago

Clauses in the Banking and Financial Dealings Act allow the government
to alter dates at short notice

A CIP record for this book is available from the British Library

ISBN 978–0–571–32779–9 (coral cover edition)
ISBN 978–0–571–32992–2 (heather cover edition)

The colours of this year's diary are taken from the jacket design for
Hugo Williams's 2009 collection, *West End Final*.

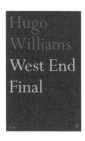

Faber & Faber

Poetry

Diary

2017

JANUARY

M	T	W	T	F	S	S
26	27	28	29	30	31	1
2	3	4	5	6	7	8
9	10	11	12	13	14	15
16	17	18	19	20	21	22
23	24	25	26	27	28	29
30	31	1	2	3	4	5

FEBRUARY

M	T	W	T	F	S	S
30	31	1	2	3	4	5
6	7	8	9	10	11	12
13	14	15	16	17	18	19
20	21	22	23	24	25	26
27	28	1	2	3	4	5
6	7	8	9	10	11	12

MARCH

M	T	W	T	F	S	S
27	28	1	2	3	4	5
6	7	8	9	10	11	12
13	14	15	16	17	18	19
20	21	22	23	24	25	26
27	28	29	30	31	1	2
3	4	5	6	7	8	9

APRIL

M	T	W	T	F	S	S
27	28	29	30	31	1	2
3	4	5	6	7	8	9
10	11	12	13	14	15	16
17	18	19	20	21	22	23
24	25	26	27	28	29	30
1	2	3	4	5	6	7

MAY

M	T	W	T	F	S	S
1	2	3	4	5	6	7
8	9	10	11	12	13	14
15	16	17	18	19	20	21
22	23	24	25	26	27	28
29	30	31	1	2	3	4
5	6	7	8	9	10	11

JUNE

M	T	W	T	F	S	S
29	30	31	1	2	3	4
5	6	7	8	9	10	11
12	13	14	15	16	17	18
19	20	21	22	23	24	25
26	27	28	29	30	1	2
3	4	5	6	7	8	9

JULY

M	T	W	T	F	S	S
26	27	28	29	30	1	2
3	4	5	6	7	8	9
10	11	12	13	14	15	16
17	18	19	20	21	22	23
24	25	26	27	28	29	30
31	1	2	3	4	5	6

AUGUST

M	T	W	T	F	S	S
31	1	2	3	4	5	6
7	8	9	10	11	12	13
14	15	16	17	18	19	20
21	22	23	24	25	26	27
28	29	30	31	1	2	3
4	5	6	7	8	9	10

SEPTEMBER

M	T	W	T	F	S	S
28	29	30	31	1	2	3
4	5	6	7	8	9	10
11	12	13	14	15	16	17
18	19	20	21	22	23	24
25	26	27	28	29	30	1
2	3	4	5	6	7	8

OCTOBER

M	T	W	T	F	S	S
25	26	27	28	29	30	1
2	3	4	5	6	7	8
9	10	11	12	13	14	15
16	17	18	19	20	21	22
23	24	25	26	27	28	29
30	31	1	2	3	4	5

NOVEMBER

M	T	W	T	F	S	S
30	31	1	2	3	4	5
6	7	8	9	10	11	12
13	14	15	16	17	18	19
20	21	22	23	24	25	26
27	28	29	30	1	2	3
4	5	6	7	8	9	10

DECEMBER

M	T	W	T	F	S	S
27	28	29	30	1	2	3
4	5	6	7	8	9	10
11	12	13	14	15	16	17
18	19	20	21	22	23	24
25	26	27	28	29	30	31
1	2	3	4	5	6	7

2016

JANUARY
M	T	W	T	F	S	S
28	29	30	31	1	2	3
4	5	6	7	8	9	10
11	12	13	14	15	16	17
18	19	20	21	22	23	24
25	26	27	28	29	30	31
1	2	3	4	5	6	7

FEBRUARY
M	T	W	T	F	S	S
25	26	27	28	29	30	31
1	2	3	4	5	6	7
8	9	10	11	12	13	14
15	16	17	18	19	20	21
22	23	24	25	26	27	28
29	1	2	3	4	5	6

MARCH
M	T	W	T	F	S	S
29	1	2	3	4	5	6
7	8	9	10	11	12	13
14	15	16	17	18	19	20
21	22	23	24	25	26	27
28	29	30	31	1	2	3
4	5	6	7	8	9	10

APRIL
M	T	W	T	F	S	S
28	29	30	31	1	2	3
4	5	6	7	8	9	10
11	12	13	14	15	16	17
18	19	20	21	22	23	24
25	26	27	28	29	30	1
2	3	4	5	6	7	8

MAY
M	T	W	T	F	S	S
25	26	27	28	29	30	1
2	3	4	5	6	7	8
9	10	11	12	13	14	15
16	17	18	19	20	21	22
23	24	25	26	27	28	29
30	31	1	2	3	4	5

JUNE
M	T	W	T	F	S	S
30	31	1	2	3	4	5
6	7	8	9	10	11	12
13	14	15	16	17	18	19
20	21	22	23	24	25	26
27	28	29	30	1	2	3
4	5	6	7	8	9	10

JULY
M	T	W	T	F	S	S
27	28	29	30	1	2	3
4	5	6	7	8	9	10
11	12	13	14	15	16	17
18	19	20	21	22	23	24
25	26	27	28	29	30	31
1	2	3	4	5	6	7

AUGUST
M	T	W	T	F	S	S
1	2	3	4	5	6	7
8	9	10	11	12	13	14
15	16	17	18	19	20	21
22	23	24	25	26	27	28
29	30	31	1	2	3	4
5	6	7	8	9	10	11

SEPTEMBER
M	T	W	T	F	S	S
29	30	31	1	2	3	4
5	6	7	8	9	10	11
12	13	14	15	16	17	18
19	20	21	22	23	24	25
26	27	28	29	30	1	2
3	4	5	6	7	8	9

OCTOBER
M	T	W	T	F	S	S
26	27	28	29	30	1	2
3	4	5	6	7	8	9
10	11	12	13	14	15	16
17	18	19	20	21	22	23
24	25	26	27	28	29	30
31	1	2	3	4	5	6

NOVEMBER
M	T	W	T	F	S	S
31	1	2	3	4	5	6
7	8	9	10	11	12	13
14	15	16	17	18	19	20
21	22	23	24	25	26	27
28	29	30	1	2	3	4
5	6	7	8	9	10	11

DECEMBER
M	T	W	T	F	S	S
28	29	30	1	2	3	4
5	6	7	8	9	10	11
12	13	14	15	16	17	18
19	20	21	22	23	24	25
26	27	28	29	30	31	1
2	3	4	5	6	7	8

2018

JANUARY
M	T	W	T	F	S	S
1	2	3	4	5	6	7
8	9	10	11	12	13	14
15	16	17	18	19	20	21
22	23	24	25	26	27	28
29	30	31	1	2	3	4
5	6	7	8	9	10	11

FEBRUARY
M	T	W	T	F	S	S
29	30	31	1	2	3	4
5	6	7	8	9	10	11
12	13	14	15	16	17	18
19	20	21	22	23	24	25
26	27	28	1	2	3	4
5	6	7	8	9	10	11

MARCH
M	T	W	T	F	S	S
26	27	28	1	2	3	4
5	6	7	8	9	10	11
12	13	14	15	16	17	18
19	20	21	22	23	24	25
26	27	28	29	30	31	1
2	3	4	5	6	7	8

APRIL
M	T	W	T	F	S	S
26	27	28	29	30	31	1
2	3	4	5	6	7	8
9	10	11	12	13	14	15
16	17	18	19	20	21	22
23	24	25	26	27	28	29
30	1	2	3	4	5	6

MAY
M	T	W	T	F	S	S
30	1	2	3	4	5	6
7	8	9	10	11	12	13
14	15	16	17	18	19	20
21	22	23	24	25	26	27
28	29	30	31	1	2	3
4	5	6	7	8	9	10

JUNE
M	T	W	T	F	S	S
28	29	30	31	1	2	3
4	5	6	7	8	9	10
11	12	13	14	15	16	17
18	19	20	21	22	23	24
25	26	27	28	29	30	1
2	3	4	5	6	7	8

JULY
M	T	W	T	F	S	S
25	26	27	28	29	30	1
2	3	4	5	6	7	8
9	10	11	12	13	14	15
16	17	18	19	20	21	22
23	24	25	26	27	28	29
30	31	1	2	3	4	5

AUGUST
M	T	W	T	F	S	S
30	31	1	2	3	4	5
6	7	8	9	10	11	12
13	14	15	16	17	18	19
20	21	22	23	24	25	26
27	28	29	30	31	1	2
3	4	5	6	7	8	9

SEPTEMBER
M	T	W	T	F	S	S
27	28	29	30	31	1	2
3	4	5	6	7	8	9
10	11	12	13	14	15	16
17	18	19	20	21	22	23
24	25	26	27	28	29	30
1	2	3	4	5	6	7

OCTOBER
M	T	W	T	F	S	S
1	2	3	4	5	6	7
8	9	10	11	12	13	14
15	16	17	18	19	20	21
22	23	24	25	26	27	28
29	30	31	1	2	3	4
5	6	7	8	9	10	11

NOVEMBER
M	T	W	T	F	S	S
29	30	31	1	2	3	4
5	6	7	8	9	10	11
12	13	14	15	16	17	18
19	20	21	22	23	24	25
26	27	28	29	30	1	2
3	4	5	6	7	8	9

DECEMBER
M	T	W	T	F	S	S
26	27	28	29	30	1	2
3	4	5	6	7	8	9
10	11	12	13	14	15	16
17	18	19	20	21	22	23
24	25	26	27	28	29	30
31	1	2	3	4	5	6

Crossing the Water

Black lake, black boat, two black, cut-paper people.
Where do the black trees go that drink here?
Their shadows must cover Canada.

A little light is filtering from the water flowers.
Their leaves do not wish us to hurry:
They are round and flat and full of dark advice.

Cold worlds shake from the oar.
The spirit of blackness is in us, it is in the fishes.
A snag is lifting a valedictory, pale hand;

Stars open among the lilies.
Are you not blinded by such expressionless sirens?
This is the silence of astounded souls.

26 Monday

27 Tuesday

28 Wednesday

29 Thursday

30 Friday

31 Saturday   NEW YEAR'S EVE   1 Sunday   NEW YEAR'S DAY

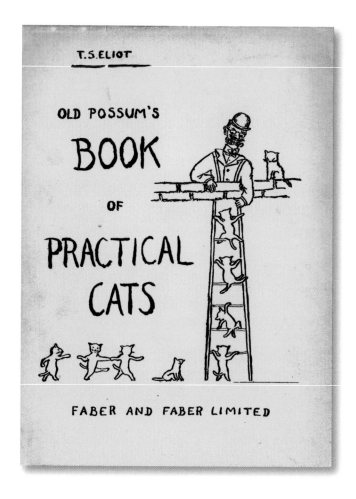

2	Monday	NEW YEAR'S DAY HOLIDAY (UK, IRL, AUS, ZA, NZ, CAN, USA)
		2ND JANUARY HOLIDAY (SCT)

3	Tuesday	DAY AFTER NEW YEAR'S DAY (NZ)
		NEW YEAR'S DAY HOLIDAY (SUBSTITUTE DAY) (SCT)

---

4 Wednesday

---

5 Thursday

---

6 Friday

---

7 Saturday   8 Sunday

Felix Randal

Felix Randal the farrier, O is he dead then? my duty all ended,
Who have watched his mould of man, big-boned and hardy-
   handsome
Pining, pining, till time when reason rambled in it and some
Fatal four disorders, fleshed there, all contended?

Sickness broke him. Impatient, he cursed at first, but mended
Being anointed and all; though a heavenlier heart began some
Months earlier, since I had our sweet reprieve and ransom
Tendered to him. Ah well, God rest him all road ever he
   offended!
This seeing the sick endears them to us, us too it endears.
My tongue had taught thee comfort, touch had quenched thy
   tears,
Thy tears that touched my heart, child, Felix, poor Felix
   Randal;

How far from then forethought of, all thy more boisterous
   years,
When thou at the random grim forge, powerful amidst peers,
Didst fettle for the great grey drayhorse his bright and
   battering sandal!

POET TO POET – *Gerard Manley Hopkins: Poems selected by John Stammers*

9 Monday

10 Tuesday

11 Wednesday

12 Thursday

13 Friday

14 Saturday   15 Sunday

Last of the Campus Poems

It's cosy in here, my seat
right next to the library window,
its panorama of snow, snow listlessly
adding itself
to already snow-daintified trees.

The computers stand idle,
inscrutable as barn owls,
and the muffled brouhaha the heating makes
makes for a very superior
brand of silence.

Term ends, and it's a poignant
satisfaction to know
that I have nothing new to say
on the subject of snow –
or, if I do have,
I am certainly not about to say it.

16 Monday   MARTIN LUTHER KING DAY (USA)

17 Tuesday

18 Wednesday

19 Thursday

20 Friday   INAUGURATION DAY

21 Saturday   22 Sunday

The Cares o' Love

HE

The cares o' Love are sweeter far
  Than onie other pleasure;
And if sae dear its sorrows are
  Enjoyment, what a treasure!

SHE

I fear to try, I dare na try
  A passion sae ensnaring;
For light's her heart and blythe's her song
  That for nae man is caring.

POET TO POET — *Robert Burns: Poems selected by Don Paterson*

23 Monday

24 Tuesday

25 Wednesday   BURNS NIGHT

26 Thursday   AUSTRALIA DAY (AUS)

27 Friday

28 Saturday   29 Sunday

Death of a Naturalist

by Seamus Heaney

ff

30 Monday

31 Tuesday

1 Wednesday

2 Thursday

3 Friday

4 Saturday   5 Sunday

Tho' hid in spiral myrtle Wreath

Tho' hid in spiral myrtle Wreath,
Love is a sword that cuts its Sheath:
And thro' the Slits, itself has made,
We spy the Glitter of the Blade.

But thro' the Slits, itself had made,
We spy no less too, that the Blade
Is eat away or snapt atwain,
And nought but Hilt and Stump remain.

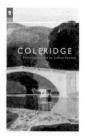

POET TO POET – *Samuel Taylor Coleridge: Poems selected by James Fenton*

6 Monday   WAITANGI DAY (NZ)

7 Tuesday

8 Wednesday

9 Thursday

10 Friday

11 Saturday

12 Sunday   LINCOLN'S BIRTHDAY

The day he died

Was the silkiest day of the young year,
The first reconnaissance of the real spring,
The first confidence of the sun.

That was yesterday. Last night, frost.
And as hard as any of all winter.
Mars and Saturn and the Moon dangling in a bunch
On the hard, littered sky.
Today is Valentine's day.

Earth toast-crisp. The snowdrops battered.
Thrushes spluttering. Pigeons gingerly
Rubbing their voices together, in stinging cold.
Crows creaking, and clumsily
Cracking loose.

The bright fields look dazed.
Their expression is changed.
They have been somewhere awful
And come back without him.

The trustful cattle, with frost on their backs,
Waiting for hay, waiting for warmth,
Stand in a new emptiness.

From now on the land
Will have to manage without him.
But it hesitates, in this slow realisation of light,
Childlike, too naked, in a frail sun,
With roots cut
And a great blank in its memory.

13 Monday

14 Tuesday VALENTINE'S DAY

15 Wednesday

16 Thursday

17 Friday

18 Saturday   19 Sunday

LAURA
RIDING

Selected
POEMS:
in Five Sets

FABER paper covered EDITIONS

20 Monday   PRESIDENTS' DAY (USA)

21 Tuesday

22 Wednesday

23 Thursday

24 Friday

25 Saturday   26 Sunday

Wood Pictures in Spring

The rich brown-umber hue the oaks unfold
When spring's young sunshine bathes their trunks in gold,
So rich, so beautiful, so past the power
Of words to paint – my heart aches for the dower
The pencil gives to soften and infuse
This brown luxuriance of unfolding hues,
This living luscious tinting woodlands give
Into a landscape that might breathe and live,
And this old gate that claps against the tree
The entrance of spring's paradise should be –
Yet paint itself with living nature fails:
The sunshine threading through these broken rails
In mellow shades no pencil e'er conveys,
And mind alone feels fancies and portrays.

27 Monday

28 Tuesday   SHROVE TUESDAY

1 Wednesday   ST DAVID'S DAY

2 Thursday

3 Friday

4 Saturday   5 Sunday

from A Shropshire Lad

XL

Into my heart an air that kills
    From yon far country blows:
What are those blue remembered hills,
    What spires, what farms are those?

That is the land of lost content,
    I see it shining plain,
The happy highways where I went
    And cannot come again.

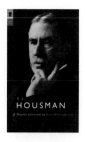

POET TO POET — *A. E. Housman: Poems selected by Alan Hollinghurst*

6 Monday

7 Tuesday

8 Wednesday

9 Thursday

10 Friday

11 Saturday   12 Sunday

Sonnet

Here it is again, spring, 'the renewal'.
People have written about this before.
And the people who track the four seasons,
the hunters who know the weather has changed.

Still, rains happen; there are slow roots that make
progress; something has a hand in the earth
and turns it. Clouds unknot the wind. Bulbs blow.
Their threadbare minds gust outward, turn yellow

eyes to heaven. It answers with the sun.
And the sun is a bulb, a mutual bomb.
The daffodils crack. 'Oh heavens!' they fret,

'Where's your terminus?' The flowers are wan
travellers. They unpack their cases. All
they know, they are. Renewal, rest. Renewal.

13 Monday

14 Tuesday

15 Wednesday

16 Thursday

17 Friday   ST PATRICK'S DAY (IRL, NI)

18 Saturday   19 Sunday

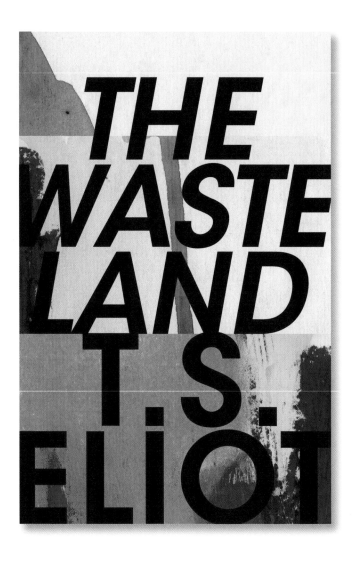

20 Monday

21 Tuesday HUMAN RIGHTS DAY (ZA)

22 Wednesday

23 Thursday

24 Friday

25 Saturday   26 Sunday

The Pulley

When God at first made man,
Having a glasse of blessings standing by,
Let us (said he) poure on him all we can:
Let the worlds riches, which dispersed lie,
    Contract into a span.

So strength first made a way;
Then beautie flow'd, then wisdome, honour, pleasure:
When almost all was out, God made a stay,
Perceiving that alone of all his treasure
    Rest in the bottome lay.

For if I should (said he)
Bestow this jewell also on my creature,
He would adore my gifts in stead of me,
And rest in Nature, not the God of Nature:
    So both should losers be.

Yet let him keep the rest,
But keep them with repining restlesnesse:
Let him be rich and wearie, that at least,
If goodnesse leade him not, yet wearinesse
    May tosse him to my breast.

POET TO POET – *George Herbert: Poems selected by Jo Shapcott*

27   Monday

28   Tuesday

29   Wednesday

30   Thursday

31   Friday

1   Saturday   2   Sunday

Paper Aeroplane

The man sitting next to me on the flight
was reading a blank book, keen eyes
panning left to right across empty leaves, fingers
turning from one white space to the next.

Sometimes he'd nod agreeably or shake his head,
or painstakingly underline some invisible text
with red ink, or decorate the margin
with an exclamation mark or asterisk.

It was a hefty-looking tome, hand-stitched
but wordless front and back and down the spine.
Coming in to land he laid the silver ribbon-marker
between two bare pages to save his place.

I was wearing noise-cancelling headphones,
listening to fine mist, when he leaned across
and shouted, 'Forgive the intrusion, but
would you sign this for me? I think it's your best.'

3 Monday

4 Tuesday

5 Wednesday

6 Thursday

7 Friday

8 Saturday

9 Sunday

There is a Garden in her face

There is a Garden in her face,
Where Roses and white Lillies grow;
A heav'nly paradice is that place,
Wherein all pleasant fruits doe flow.
There Cherries grow, which none may buy
Till Cherry ripe themselves doe cry.

Those Cherries fayrely doe enclose
Of Orient Pearle a double row,
Which when her lovely laughter showes,
They looke like Rose-buds fill'd with snow.
Yet them nor Peere nor Prince can buy,
Till Cherry ripe themselves doe cry.

Her Eyes like Angels watch them still;
Her Browes like bended bowes doe stand,
Threatning with piercing frownes to kill
All that attempt with eye or hand
Those sacred Cherries to come nigh,
Till Cherry ripe themselves doe cry.

10 Monday

11 Tuesday

12 Wednesday

13 Thursday

14 Friday   GOOD FRIDAY (UK, AUS, ZA, NZ, CAN)

15 Saturday   EASTER (HOLY) SATURDAY   16 Sunday   EASTER SUNDAY (NZ)

SYLVIA
PLATH
Poems
chosen by
CAROL ANN
DUFFY

17 **Monday** EASTER MONDAY (UK NOT SCT, IRL, AUS, NZ)
TAX DAY: USA, FAMILY DAY (ZA)

18 Tuesday

19 Wednesday

20 Thursday

21 Friday

22 Saturday

23 **Sunday** ST GEORGE'S DAY

M.A.D. 1971 (Rat-run)

It will be the rat, he told her, the rat that first emerges from the crud
and crap after the infinite rapture of the megaton strike, its head
slick with what it burrowed through, what fell, what kept it fed.

You and I will close and fuse, bone seared to bone, flesh folded in.
Our silhouette will print the wall, one subterfuge, one skin.
Joined as never before, but joined, as we would have wished, in sin.

*

There were men in the seas of the moon. The great hare lay dead.
What they seemed to speak were broken lines of some unbroken code.
What they seemed to hear was the voice of God howling in the void.

Earth was a rolling abstract, its blue-white trappings dense
in darkness. They named it *terra nullius*. They were drenched
in starlight, dead light. They scuffed the dust as they danced.

*

It's nine, he told her, can you see? Nine, which multiplied
by any number reduces again to nine — vows of the woodland bride,
choirs of angels, fleshly portals, nine versions of the road

to Gethsemane . . . Bad luck, of course, to dream in nines
but it can only have been in sleep that I saw them, rat-clones
in a whirlwind of ash, the city burn-out, the broken stones.

24 Monday

25 Tuesday

26 Wednesday   ANZAC DAY (AUS, NZ)

27 Thursday   FREEDOM DAY (ZA)

28 Friday

29 Saturday   30 Sunday

Drowing is not so pitiful

Drowning is not so pitiful
As the attempt to rise.
Three times, 'tis said, a sinking man
Comes up to face the skies,
And then declines forever
To that abhorred abode,
Where hope and he part company—
For he is grasped of God.
The Maker's cordial visage,
However good to see,
Is shunned, we must admit it,
Like an adversity.

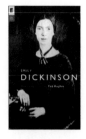

1 Monday WORKERS' DAY (ZA) EARLY MAY BANK HOLIDAY (UK)
MAY DAY (IRL)

2 Tuesday

3 Wednesday

4 Thursday

5 Friday

6 Saturday   7 Sunday

from Ramayana: A Retelling

Rama's second take
on who is that, is that
   the beauty of the world
      across on the balcony
         observing the jamboree . . . ?
       And her eyes fell
according to the exact second of the cosmic dial
        that we call fate,
    on Rama's eyes
   at the same time
  as Rama's had flown
startled upon hers.

Their heartbeats doubled on the same count
   and harkened in a shared breath.

The harkening damsel was
   Sita

who was taking in her familiar Mithilan view
when she fell on a feeling of greater familiarity
punctuated by the sorrow of utter unknowing.

Whilst Rama dazed at her beauty, Sita dazed at his

and thought to herself how this must be
the veiled recognition
   that we call love at first sight.

Together they had walked, aeon after aeon,
fresh as bold new lovers, under the starry lanes
   in heaven:
he as Vishnu and she as Lakshmi.

8 Monday

9 Tuesday

10 Wednesday

11 Thursday

12 Friday

13 Saturday   14 Sunday

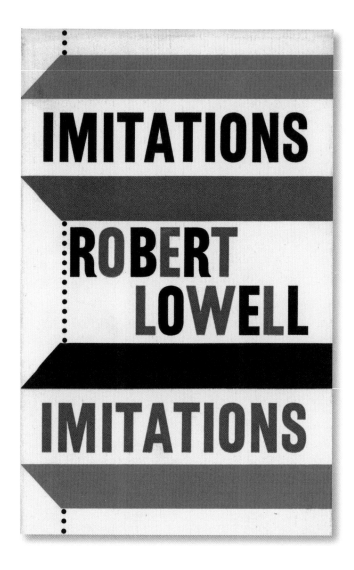

15 Monday

16 Tuesday

17 Wednesday

18 Thursday

19 Friday

20 Saturday   21 Sunday

Another Unfortunate Choice

I think I am in love with A. E. Housman,
Which puts me in a worse-than-usual fix.
No woman ever stood a chance with Housman
And he's been dead since 1936.

22 Monday

23 Tuesday

24 Wednesday

25 Thursday

26 Friday

27 Saturday   28 Sunday

He wishes for the Cloths of Heaven

Had I the heavens' embroidered cloths,
Enwrought with golden and silver light,
The blue and the dim and the dark cloths
Of night and light and the half-light,
I would spread the cloths under your feet:
But I, being poor, have only my dreams;
I have spread my dreams under your feet;
Tread softly because you tread on my dreams.

POET TO POET — *W. B. Yeats: Poems selected by Seamus Heaney*

29 **Monday**

30 Tuesday

31 Wednesday

1 Thursday

2 Friday

3 Saturday

4 Sunday

The Triple Foole

I am two fooles, I know,
For loving, and for saying so
    In whining Poëtry;
But where's that wiseman, that would not be I,
    If she would not deny?
Then as th'earths inward narrow crooked lanes
Do purge sea waters fretfull salt away,
    I thought, if I could draw my paines,
Through Rimes vexation, I should them allay,
Griefe brought to numbers cannot be so fierce,
For, he tames it, that fetters it in verse.

But when I have done so,
Some man, his art and voice to show,
    Doth Set and sing my paine,
And, by delighting many, frees againe
    Griefe, which verse did restraine.
To Love, and Griefe tribute of Verse belongs,
But not of such as pleases when'tis read,
    Both are increased by such songs:
For both their triumphs so are published,
And I, which was two fooles, do so grow three;
Who are a little wise, the best fooles bee.

POET TO POET – *John Donne: Poems selected by Paul Muldoon*

5 Monday <small>JUNE BANK HOLIDAY (IRL) QUEEN'S BIRTHDAY HOLIDAY (NZ)</small>

6 Tuesday

7 Wednesday

8 Thursday

9 Friday

10 Saturday   11 Sunday

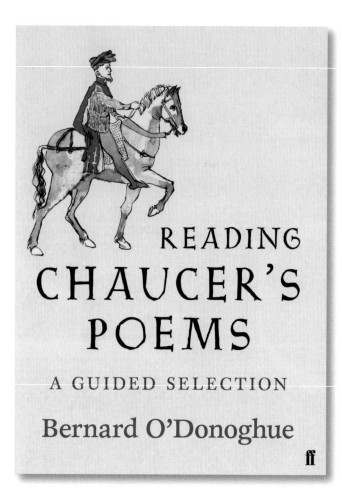

READING
CHAUCER'S
POEMS

A GUIDED SELECTION

Bernard O'Donoghue

ff

1 2   Monday

_____

1 3   Tuesday

_____

1 4   Wednesday

_____

1 5   Thursday

_____

1 6   Friday   YOUTH DAY (ZA)

_____

1 7   Saturday   1 8   Sunday

Kata

A dance between movement and space,
between image and imperative.
Each step an arrival
of the familiar within the unknown.
The gravity of form
and the mechanism of each gesture
as profound and dissolved
as the body's memory of a stranger
who said nothing but in passing
met with you in stillness
wanting to go no faster than this.

19 Monday

20 Tuesday

21 Wednesday

22 Thursday

23 Friday

24 Saturday   25 Sunday

The succession of the foure sweet months

First, April, she with mellow showrs
Opens the way for early flowers;
Then after her comes smiling May,
In a more rich and sweet aray:
Next enters June, and brings us more
Jems, then those two, that went before:
Then (lastly) July comes, and she
More wealth brings in, then all those three.

POET TO POET — *Robert Herrick: Poems selected by Stephen Romer*

26 Monday

27 Tuesday

28 Wednesday

29 Thursday

30 Friday

1 Saturday   CANADA DAY   2 Sunday

My Oak

has memory: it put the wind which shook
the sapling into the mass of its trunk;
it put the prevalence of weather
down Hanter Hill into its weighted curve
across the skyline; that infestation
of caterpillars was remembered by the leaves
which contracted and thickened the next year.
It remembers the seasons, or at least the length
of darknesses which distinguish them:
our word is photoperiodism, but remember
is not the word, nor is it my oak although
I used to watch it every day, when
I lived across the field, watch it
respond to everything, everything else.

3 Monday CANADA DAY HOLIDAY (CAN)

4 Tuesday INDEPENDENCE DAY (USA)

5 Wednesday

6 Thursday

7 Friday

8 Saturday   9 Sunday

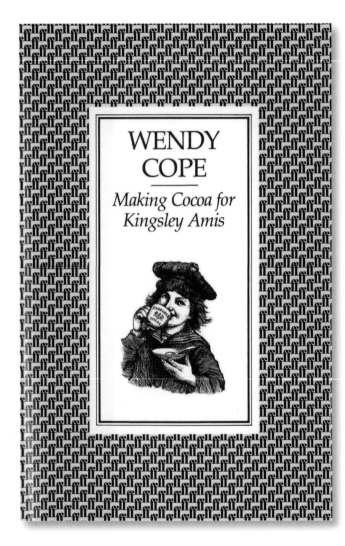

WENDY
COPE
———
*Making Cocoa for
Kingsley Amis*

10 Monday

11 Tuesday

12 Wednesday   BATTLE OF THE BOYNE HOLIDAY (NI)

13 Thursday

14 Friday

15 Saturday   16 Sunday

A Porcupine

Simply because she'd turn her back on me,
a porcupine on the Homer Noble farm
would unwittingly
give me a shot in the arm,

bustling off in her ball gown
while clutching a quillwork purse.
I'm thinking how our need to do ourselves down
will often be in inverse

proportion to how much we want
to be esteemed. I'm thinking of those who,
in the same breath, will kiss up to us and kiss

us off. I'm thinking of a woman who'd flaunt
from her shoulder blade a tattoo:
I REGRET THIS.

17 Monday

18 Tuesday

19 Wednesday

20 Thursday

21 Friday

22 Saturday   23 Sunday

An Exhortation

Chameleons feed on light and air:
    Poets' food is love and fame:
If in this wide world of care
    Poets could but find the same
With as little toil as they,
    Would they ever change their hue
    As the light chameleons do,
Suiting it to every ray
    Twenty times a day?

Poets are on this cold earth,
    As chameleons might be,
Hidden from their early birth
    In a cave beneath the sea;
Where light is, chameleons change:
    Where love is not, poets do:
    Fame is love disguised: if few
Find either, never think it strange
    That poets range.

Yet dare not stain with wealth or power
    A poet's free and heavenly mind:
If bright chameleons should devour
    Any food but beams and wind,
They would grow as earthly soon
    As their brother lizards are.
    Children of a sunnier star,
Spirits from beyond the moon,
    O, refuse the boon!

POET TO POET – *Percy Bysshe Shelley: Poems selected by Fiona Sampson*

4 Monday

5 Tuesday

6 Wednesday

7 Thursday

8 Friday

9 Saturday   30 Sunday

La Figlia Che Piange

O quam te memorem virgo . . .

Stand on the highest pavement of the stair—
Lean on a garden urn—
Weave, weave the sunlight in your hair—
Clasp your flowers to you with a pained surprise—
Fling them to the ground and turn
With a fugitive resentment in your eyes:
But weave, weave the sunlight in your hair.

So I would have had him leave,
So I would have had her stand and grieve,
So he would have left
As the soul leaves the body torn and bruised,
As the mind deserts the body it has used.
I should find
Some way incomparably light and deft,
Some way we both should understand,
Simple and faithless as a smile and shake of the hand.

She turned away, but with the autumn weather
Compelled my imagination many days,
Many days and many hours:
Her hair over her arms and her arms full of flowers.
And I wonder how they should have been together!
I should have lost a gesture and a pose.
Sometimes these cogitations still amaze
The troubled midnight and the noon's repose.

31 Monday

1 Tuesday

2 Wednesday

3 Thursday

4 Friday

5 Saturday   6 Sunday

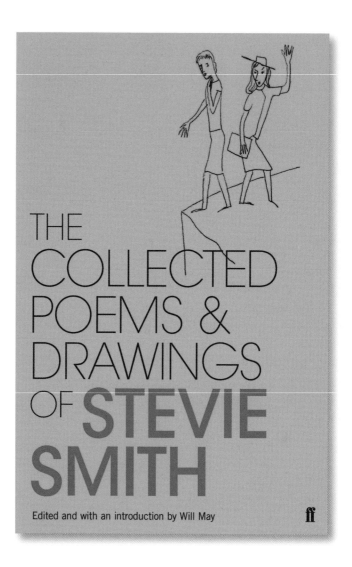

THE
COLLECTED
POEMS &
DRAWINGS
OF STEVIE
SMITH

Edited and with an introduction by Will May

ff

7 Monday SUMMER BANK HOLIDAY (SCT, IRL)

8 Tuesday

9 Wednesday NATIONAL WOMEN'S DAY HOLIDAY (ZA)

10 Thursday

11 Friday

12 Saturday   13 Sunday

Now Sleeps the Crimson Petal

Now sleeps the crimson petal, now the white;
Nor waves the cypress in the palace walk;
Nor winks the gold fin in the porphyry font:
The fire-fly wakens: waken thou with me.

Now droops the milkwhite peacock like a ghost,
And like a ghost she glimmers on to me.

Now lies the Earth all Danaë to the stars,
And all thy heart lies open unto me.

Now slides the silent meteor on, and leaves
A shining furrow, as thy thoughts in me.

Now folds the lily all her sweetness up,
And slips into the bosom of the lake:
So fold thyself, my dearest, thou, and slip
Into my bosom and be lost in me.

POET TO POET — *Alfred, Lord Tennyson: Poems selected by Mick Imlah*

14 Monday

15 Tuesday

16 Wednesday

17 Thursday

18 Friday

19 Saturday   20 Sunday

The Underground

There we were in the vaulted tunnel running,
You in your going-away coat speeding ahead
And me, me then like a fleet god gaining
Upon you before you turned to a reed

Or some new white flower japped with crimson
As the coat flapped wild and button after button
Sprang off and fell in a trail
Between the Underground and the Albert Hall.

Honeymooning, mooning around, late for the Proms,
Our echoes die in that corridor and now
I come as Hansel came on the moonlit stones
Retracing the path back, lifting the buttons

To end up in a draughty lamplit station
After the trains have gone, the wet track
Bared and tensed as I am, all attention
For your step following and damned if I look back.

21 Monday   Friendship Lane · PSychiatrist 11 AM

22 Tuesday

23 Wednesday

24 Thursday

25 Friday

26 Saturday   27 Sunday

Shy Willows

The swallows diving and crying
above the streets and squares
picking and unpicking their threads
– sewing nothing with nothing
then the sallows the sallies the gardens
– river gardens –
I want their greens and their ochres
against those blue and white buildings
and I want the term *shaggy*
– not so far from *savage* –
soaked into its silks

28 Monday   SUMMER BANK HOLIDAY (UK NOT SCT)

29 Tuesday

30 Wednesday

31 Thursday

1 Friday

2 Saturday   3 Sunday

W. H. AUDEN

Selected POEMS

FABER paper covered EDITIONS

4 **Monday** LABOR DAY (USA) LABOUR DAY (CAN)

5 Tuesday

6 Wednesday

7 Thursday

8 Friday

9 Saturday   10 Sunday

The Human Seasons

Four Seasons fill the measure of the year;
    There are four seasons in the mind of man:
He has his lusty Spring, when fancy clear
    Takes in all beauty with an easy span:
He has his Summer, when luxuriously
    Spring's honied cud of youthful thought he loves
To ruminate, and by such dreaming high
    Is nearest unto heaven: quiet coves
His soul has in its Autumn, when his wings
    He furleth close; contented so to look
On mists in idleness – to let fair things
    Pass by unheeded as a threshold brook.
He has his Winter too of pale misfeature,
Or else he would forego his mortal nature.

Poetry Please: The Seasons

1 Monday

2 Tuesday

3 Wednesday

4 Thursday

5 Friday

6 Saturday   17 Sunday

Blackdown Song

In front of the gate whose tubes hummed in the wind
like owls hooing each other across a dark field, Isabel,
was the firepit's tract of soot-soft & snow-white ashes.

It went deeper than you knew, after years of bonfires,
dusks when sightly wings of paper flared in a woosh
of sparks & ghosted into darkness like minor stars.

Beyond the singing gate lay the dark field which ate
the bodies of lambs & threw up the bleached fans
of pigeon wings: the grass grew red in those places.

I dug the pit with a shovel & scooped bucketloads
to feed my father's garden which drew down silver
mouthfuls of ash & the tangled brown potato haulms.

All the while the gate hummed tunelessly in the wind:
tunelessly, but with range: high & low, long & short,
disconnected, artless, dumb life struggling into song.

I struck so reckless, Isabel – hot, one-handed, peeved,
& clanged a rock that hung in earth as consciousness
is said to inhere in the self, the self to hang in the body.

High, low, long, short. My arms went dead, a dazed bird
burst from my skull – the rock humped, deaf to the blow.
A brilliant ringing in the blade secured itself to that axis.

18 Monday

19 Tuesday

20 Wednesday

21 Thursday   ROSH HASHANAH

22 Friday

23 Saturday   24 Sunday   HERITAGE DAY (ZA)

Digging

Today I think
Only with scents, – scents dead leaves yield,
And bracken, and wild carrot's seed,
And the square mustard field;

Odours that rise
When the spade wounds the root of tree,
Rose, currant, raspberry, or goutweed,
Rhubarb or celery;

The smoke's smell, too,
Flowing from where a bonfire burns
The dead, the waste, the dangerous,
And all to sweetness turns.

It is enough
To smell, to crumble the dark earth.
While the robin sings over again
Sad songs of Autumn mirth.

25 **Monday** HERITAGE DAY HOLIDAY (ZA)

26 Tuesday

27 Wednesday

28 Thursday

29 Friday

30 **Saturday** YOM KIPPUR   1 **Sunday**

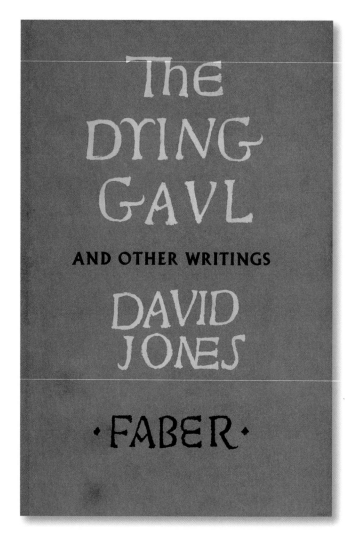

2 Monday

3 Tuesday

4 Wednesday

5 Thursday

6 Friday

7 Saturday · 8 Sunday

The Conclusion of Joseph Turrill

Garsington, Oxfordshire, 1867

I suppose I was cut out for a quiet life;
whether I have managed any such thing
is another matter,
what with larks to shoot,
and harvesting, gooseberries, and whatnot.

Then there was all that with Netty:
would she or wouldn't she;
did I or didn't I?
It is my belief
I spent more hours kicking my heels at her gate
than happy the other side.

Be that as it may.
Anno Domini drives out stern matters of fact,
and faults that appear to us
when we compare the lives we have
with those we imagine . . .
There's nothing a gentle stroll
in the woods by moonlight can't put right.

I tried that just now.
I saw swallows on the branches like clothes pegs,
which put me in such good humour
I brought home one of their nests and also four chicks.

9 Monday THANKSGIVING DAY (CAN) COLUMBUS DAY (USA)

10 Tuesday

11 Wednesday

12 Thursday

13 Friday

14 Saturday   15 Sunday

'That time of year thou mayst in me behold'

That time of year thou mayst in me behold
When yellow leaves, or none, or few, do hang
Upon those boughs which shake against the cold,
Bare ruin'd choirs, where late the sweet birds sang.
In me thou see'st the twilight of such day
As after sunset fadeth in the west;
Which by and by black night doth take away,
Death's second self that seals up all in rest.
In me thou see'st the glowing of such fire,
That on the ashes of his youth doth lie,
As the death-bed whereon it must expire
Consum'd with that which it was nourish'd by.
This thou perceiv'st, which makes thy love more
    strong,
To love that well which thou must leave ere long.

16 Monday

17 Tuesday

18 Wednesday

19 Thursday

20 Friday

21 Saturday

22 Sunday

The Roundabout

for Jamie and Russ

It's moving still, that wooden roundabout
we found at the field's end, sunk in the grass
like an ancient buckler from the giants' war.
The first day of good weather, our first out
after me and your mother. Its thrawn mass
was like trying to push a tree over, or row
a galley sealed in ice. I was all for
giving up when we felt it give, and go.
What had saved the axle all those years?
It let out one great drawn-out yawn and swung
away like a hundred gates. Our hands still burning
we lay and looked up at a sky so clear
there was nothing in the world to prove our turning
but our light heads, and the wind's lung.

23 **Monday**   LABOUR DAY (NZ)

24 Tuesday

25 Wednesday

26 Thursday

27 Friday

28 Saturday   29 Sunday

30 **Monday**   OCTOBER BANK HOLIDAY (IRL)

31 **Tuesday**   HALLOWEEN

1 Wednesday

2 Thursday

3 Friday

4 Saturday   5 Sunday

Dulce et Decorum Est

Bent double, like old beggars under sacks,
Knock-kneed, coughing like hags, we cursed through sludge,
Till on the haunting flares we turned our backs
And towards our distant rest began to trudge.
Men marched asleep. Many had lost their boots
But limped on, blood-shod. All went lame; all blind;
Drunk with fatigue; deaf even to the hoots
Of tired, outstripped Five-Nines that dropped behind.

Gas! GAS! Quick, boys! – An ecstasy of fumbling,
Fitting the clumsy helmets just in time;
But someone still was yelling out and stumbling,
And flound'ring like a man in fire or lime . . .
Dim, through the misty panes and thick green light,
As under a green sea, I saw him drowning.

In all my dreams, before my helpless sight,
He plunges at me, guttering, choking, drowning.

If in some smothering dreams you too could pace
Behind the wagon that we flung him in,
And watch the white eyes writhing in his face,
His hanging face, like a devil's sick of sin;
If you could hear, at every jolt, the blood
Come gargling from the froth-corrupted lungs,
Obscene as cancer, bitter as the cud
Of vile, incurable sores on innocent tongues, –
My friend, you would not tell with such high zest
To children ardent for some desperate glory,
The old Lie: Dulce et decorum est
Pro patria mori.

Monday

Tuesday

Wednesday

Thursday

o Friday

11 Saturday   REMEMBRANCE DAY   12 Sunday   REMEMBRANCE SUNDAY
             (CAN)

'The spell is broke, the charm is flown!'

Written at Athens, January 16, 1810

The spell is broke, the charm is flown!
    Thus is it with life's fitful fever:
We madly smile when we should groan:
    Delirium is our best deceiver.

Each lucid interval of thought
    Recalls the woes of Nature's charter;
And he that acts as wise men ought,
    But lives, as saints have died, a martyr.

POET TO POET – *Lord Byron: Poems selected by Paul Muldoon*

13 Monday

14 Tuesday

15 Wednesday

16 Thursday

17 Friday

18 Saturday   19 Sunday

Friday Night in the Royal Station Hotel

Light spreads darkly downwards from the high
Clusters of lights over empty chairs
That face each other, coloured differently.
Through open doors, the dining-room declares
A larger loneliness of knives and glass
And silence laid like carpet. A porter reads
An unsold evening paper. Hours pass,
And all the salesmen have gone back to Leeds,
Leaving full ashtrays in the Conference Room.

In shoeless corridors, the lights burn. How
Isolated, like a fort, it is –
The headed paper, made for writing home
(If home existed) letters of exile: *Now
Night comes on. Waves fold behind villages.*

20 Monday

21 Tuesday

22 Wednesday

23 Thursday THANKSGIVING DAY (USA)

24 Friday

25 Saturday   26 Sunday

JOHN BERRYMAN

HIS TOY
HIS DREAM
HIS REST

27 Monday

28 Tuesday

29 Wednesday

30 Thursday ST ANDREW'S DAY HOLIDAY (SCT)

1 Friday

2 Saturday 3 Sunday

Animal Tranquillity and Decay

The little hedgerow birds,
That peck along the road, regard him not.
He travels on, and in his face, his step,
His gait, is one expression: every limb,
His look and bending figure, all bespeak
A man who does not move with pain, but moves
With thought. – He is insensibly subdued
To settled quiet: he is one by whom
All effort seems forgotten; one to whom
Long patience hath such mild composure given,
That patience now doth seem a thing of which
He hath no need. He is by nature led
To peace so perfect that the young behold
With envy, what the Old Man hardly feels.

POET TO POET — *William Wordsworth: Poems selected by Seamus Heaney*

4 Monday

---

5 Tuesday

---

6 Wednesday

---

7 Thursday

---

8 Friday

---

9 Saturday   10 Sunday

A Jelly-Fish

Visible, invisible,
A fluctuating charm,
An amber-colored amethyst
Inhabits it; your arm
Approaches, and
It opens and
It closes;
You have meant
To catch it,
And it shrivels;
You abandon
Your intent –
It opens, and it
Closes and you
Reach for it –
The blue
Surrounding it
Grows cloudy, and
It floats away
From you.

11 Monday

12 Tuesday

13 Wednesday   HANUKKAH (FIRST DAY)

14 Thursday

15 Friday

16 Saturday   DAY OF
              RECONCILIATION (ZA)

17 Sunday

The Fly

Little Fly
Thy summers play,
My thoughtless hand
Has brush'd away.

Am not I
A fly like thee?
Or art not thou
A man like me?

For I dance
And drink & sing;
Till some blind hand
Shall brush my wing.

If thought is life
And strength & breath;
And the want
Of thought is death;

Then am I
A happy fly,
If I live,
Or if I die.

POET TO POET — *William Blake: Poems selected by James Fenton*

18 Monday

___

19 Tuesday

___

20 Wednesday

___

21 Thursday

___

22 Friday

___

23 Saturday

24 Sunday CHRISTMAS EVE

THE POETRY OF W.B. YEATS

BY LOUIS MACNEICE

With a Foreword
by Richard Ellmann

25 **Monday** CHRISTMAS DAY (UK, IRL, AUS, NZ, ZA, CAN, USA)

26 Tuesday BOXING DAY (UK, AUS, NZ)
ST STEPHEN'S DAY (IRL) DAY OF GOODWILL (ZA)

27 Wednesday

28 Thursday

29 Friday

30 Saturday   31 **Sunday** NEW YEAR'S EVE

A Brief Chronology of Faber's Poetry Publishing

1925 Geoffrey Faber acquires an interest in The Scientific Press and renames the firm Faber and Gwyer. ¶ The poet/bank clerk T. S. Eliot is recruited. 'What will impress my directors favourably is the sense that in you we have found a man who combines literary gifts with business instincts.' – Geoffrey Faber to T. S. Eliot ¶ Eliot brought with him The Criterion, the quarterly periodical he had been editing since 1922. (The Waste Land had appeared in its first issue, brilliantly establishing its reputation.) He continued to edit it from the Faber offices until it closed in 1939. Though unprofitable, it was hugely influential, introducing early work by Auden, Empson and Spender, among others, and promoting many notable European writers, including Proust and Valéry. ¶ Publication of T. S. Eliot's Poems, 1909–1925, which included The Waste Land and a new sequence, The Hollow Men. ¶

1927 From 1927 to 1931 Faber publishes a series of illustrated pamphlets known as The Ariel Poems containing unpublished poems by an eminent poet (Thomas Hardy, W. B. Yeats, Harold Monro, Edith Sitwell and Edmund Blunden to name but a few) along with an illustration, usually in colour, by a leading contemporary artist (including Eric Gill, Eric Ravilious, Paul Nash and Graham Sutherland). ¶

1928 Faber and Gwyer announce the Selected Poems of Ezra Pound, with an introduction and notes by Eliot. ¶

1929 Geoffrey Faber buys out Lady Gwyer and oversees the birth of the Faber and Faber imprint. Legend has it that Walter de la Mare, the father of Faber director Richard de la Mare, suggested the euphonious repetition: another Faber in the company name 'because you can't have too much of a good thing'. ¶

1930 W. H. Auden becomes a Faber poet with a collection entitled simply Poems. ¶ Eliot publishes Ash Wednesday. ¶

1933 Stephen Spender becomes a Faber poet with his first collection Poems, a companion piece to Auden's 1930 work of the same name. ¶ The first British edition of James Joyce's Pomes Penyeach is published. ¶

1935 The American poet Marianne Moore publishes with Faber. 'Miss Moore's poems form part of a small body of durable poetry written in our time.' – T. S. Eliot ¶ Louis MacNeice becomes a Faber poet. 'The most original Irish poet of his generation.' – Faber catalogue 1935 ¶

1936 The hugely influential Faber Book of Modern Verse (edited by Michael Roberts) is published. ¶

1937 *In Parenthesis* by David Jones is published. 'This is an epic of war. But it is like no other war-book because for the first time that experience has been reduced to "a shape in words." The impression still remains that this book is one of the most remarkable literary achievements of our time.' – *Times Literary Supplement* ¶ W. H. Auden is awarded the Queen's Gold Medal for Poetry. ¶

1939 T. S. Eliot's *Old Possum's Book of Practical Cats* is published with a book jacket illustrated by the author. Originally called *Pollicle Dogs and Jellicle Cats*, the poems were written for his five godchildren. The eldest of these was Geoffrey Faber's son Tom – himself much later a director of Faber and Faber. ¶

1944 Walter de la Mare's *Peacock Pie* is published with illustrations by Edward Ardizzone. ¶ Philip Larkin's first novel, *A Girl in Winter*, is published. 'A young man with an exceptionally clear sense of what, as a writer, he means to do.' – *Times Literary Supplement* ¶

1948 T. S. Eliot wins the Nobel Prize in Literature. ¶

1949 Ezra Pound's *Pisan Cantos* is published. 'The most incomprehensible passages are often more stimulating than much comprehensibility which passes for poetry today.' – *Times Literary Supplement* ¶

1954 *The Ariel Poems* are revived with a new set of pamphlets by W. H. Auden, Stephen Spender, Louis MacNeice, T. S. Eliot, Walter de la Mare, Cecil Day Lewis and Roy Campbell. The artists include Edward Ardizzone, Edward Bawden, Michael Ayrton and John Piper. ¶

1957 Ted Hughes comes to Faber with *The Hawk in the Rain*. ¶ Siegfried Sassoon receives the Queen's Gold Medal for Poetry. ¶

1959 Robert Lowell's collection *Life Studies* is published. ¶

1960 Saint-John Perse wins the Nobel Prize in Literature. ¶

1961 Geoffrey Faber dies. ¶ Ted Hughes's first collection of children's poems, *Meet My Folks*, is published. ¶

1963 Sylvia Plath's novel *The Bell Jar* is published by Faber in the year of her death. ¶ The Geoffrey Faber Memorial Prize is established as an annual prize awarded in alternating years to a single volume of poetry or fiction by a Commonwealth author under forty. ¶

1964 Philip Larkin's *The Whitsun Weddings* is published. ¶

1965 T. S. Eliot dies. ¶ Sylvia Plath's posthumous collection, *Ariel*, is published. 'Her extraordinary achievement, poised as she was between volatile emotional state and the edge of the precipice.' – Frieda Hughes ¶ Philip Larkin is awarded the Queen's Gold Medal for Poetry. ¶

1966 Seamus Heaney comes to Faber with *Death of a Naturalist*. ¶

1968 Ted Hughes's *The Iron Man* is published. ¶

1971 Stephen Spender is awarded the Queen's Gold Medal for Poetry. ¶

1973 Paul Muldoon comes to Faber with his first collection, *New Weather*. ¶

1974 Ted Hughes receives the Queen's Gold Medal for Poetry. ¶

1977 Tom Paulin comes to Faber with his first collection, *A State of Justice*. ¶ Norman Nicholson receives the Queen's Gold Medal for Poetry. ¶

1980 Czesław Miłosz wins the Nobel Prize in Literature. ¶

1981 *Cats*, the Andrew Lloyd Webber musical based on *Old Possum's Book of Practical Cats*, opens in London. ¶

1984 *Rich*, a collection by Faber's own poetry editor, Craig Raine, is published. 'Puts us in touch with life as unexpectedly and joyfully as early Pasternak.' – John Bayley ¶ Ted Hughes becomes Poet Laureate. ¶

1985 Douglas Dunn's collection *Elegies* is the Whitbread Book of the Year. ¶

1986 Vikram Seth's *The Golden Gate* is published. ¶

1987 Seamus Heaney's *The Haw Lantern* wins the Whitbread Poetry Award. ¶

1988 Derek Walcott is awarded the Queen's Gold Medal for Poetry. ¶

1992 Derek Walcott wins the Nobel Prize in Literature. ¶ Thom Gunn's collection *The Man with the Night Sweats* wins the Forward Poetry Prize for Best Collection, while Simon Armitage's *Kid* wins Best First Collection. ¶

1993 Andrew Motion wins the Whitbread Biography Award for his book on Philip Larkin. ¶ Don Paterson's *Nil Nil* wins the Forward Poetry Prize for Best First Collection. ¶

1994 Paul Muldoon wins the T. S. Eliot Prize for *The Annals of Chile*. ¶ Alice Oswald wins an Eric Gregory Award. ¶

1995 Seamus Heaney wins the Nobel Prize in Literature. ¶

1996 Wisława Szymborska wins the Nobel Prize in Literature. ¶ Seamus Heaney's *The Spirit Level* wins the Whitbread Poetry Award. 'Touched by a sense of wonder.' – Blake Morrison ¶

997 Don Paterson wins the T. S. Eliot Prize for *God's Gift to Women*. ¶ Lavinia Greenlaw wins the Forward Prize for Best Single Poem for 'A World Where News Travelled Slowly'. ¶ Ted Hughes's *Tales from Ovid* is the Whitbread Book of the Year. 'A breathtaking book.' – John Carey ¶

998 Ted Hughes wins the Whitbread Book of the Year for the second time running with *Birthday Letters*, which also wins the T. S. Eliot Prize. 'Language like lava, its molten turmoils hardening into jagged shapes.' – John Carey ¶ Ted Hughes is awarded the Order of Merit. ¶ Christopher Logue receives the Wilfred Owen Poetry Award. ¶

999 Seamus Heaney's *Beowulf* wins the Whitbread Book of the Year Award. '[Heaney is the] one living poet who can rightly claim to be Beowulf's heir.' – *New York Times* ¶ A memorial service for Ted Hughes is held at Westminster Abbey. In his speech Seamus Heaney calls Hughes 'a guardian spirit of the land and language'. ¶ Hugo Williams wins the T. S. Eliot Prize for his collection *Billy's Rain*. ¶ Andrew Motion is appointed Poet Laureate. ¶

000 Seamus Heaney receives the Wilfred Owen Poetry Award. ¶

002 Alice Oswald wins the T. S. Eliot Prize for Poetry for her collection *Dart*. ¶

2003 Paul Muldoon is awarded the Pulitzer Prize for Poetry for *Moy Sand and Gravel*. *Landing Light* by Don Paterson wins the Whitbread Poetry Award. ¶

2004 August Kleinzahler receives the International Griffin Prize for *The Strange Hours Travellers Keep*. ¶ Hugo Williams is awarded the Queen's Gold Medal for Poetry. ¶

2005 David Harsent wins the Forward Prize for Best Collection for *Legion*. ¶ Harold Pinter receives the Wilfred Owen Poetry Award. ¶ Charles Simic receives the International Griffin Prize for *Selected Poems 1963–2003*. ¶ Nick Laird wins an Eric Gregory Award. ¶

2006 Christopher Logue wins the Whitbread Poetry Award for *Cold Calls*. ¶ The Geoffrey Faber Memorial Prize is awarded to Alice Oswald for *Woods Etc.* ¶ Seamus Heaney wins the T. S. Eliot Prize for *District and Circle*. ¶

2007 Tony Harrison is awarded the Wilfred Owen Poetry Award. ¶ Daljit Nagra wins the Forward Prize for Best First Collection for *Look We Have Coming to Dover!* ¶ James Fenton receives the Queen's Gold Medal for Poetry. ¶

2008 Daljit Nagra wins the South Bank Show / Arts Council Decibel Award. ¶ Mick Imlah's collection *The Lost Leader* wins the Forward Prize for Best Collection. ¶

2009 Carol Ann Duffy becomes Poet Laureate. ¶ Don Paterson's *Rain* wins the Forward Poetry Prize for Best Collection while *The Striped World* by Emma Jones wins the Best First Collection Prize. ¶

2010 *The Song of Lunch* by Christopher Reid is shortlisted for the Ted Hughes Award for New Work in Poetry and he is awarded the Costa Poetry Award for *A Scattering.* ¶ The John Florio Prize for Italian Translation 2010 is awarded to Jamie McKendrick for *The Embrace.* ¶ Derek Walcott wins both the Warwick Prize and the T. S. Eliot Prize for Poetry for his collection *White Egrets.* ¶ *Rain* by Don Paterson is shortlisted for the Saltire Scottish Book of the Year. ¶ Tony Harrison is awarded the Prix Européen de Littérature. ¶ The Keats–Shelley Prize is awarded to Simon Armitage for his poem 'The Present'. ¶ The Forward Prize for Best Collection is awarded to Seamus Heaney for *Human Chain.* ¶ Also shortlisted for the Forward Prize for Best Collection are Lachlan Mackinnon for *Small Hours* and Jo Shapcott for *Of Mutability.* ¶ The Centre for Literacy in Primary Education (CLPE) Poetry Prize is awarded to Carol Ann Duffy for *New and Collected Poems for Children.* ¶ Alice Oswald wins the Ted Hughes Award for New Work in Poetry for *Weeds and Wild Flowers.* ¶ *The Striped World* by Emma Jones is shortlisted for the Adelaide Festival Poetry Award. ¶ The Queen's Gold Medal for Poetry is awarded to Don Paterson. ¶

2011 *Of Mutability* by Jo Shapcott is the Costa Book of the Year. ¶ *Human Chain* by Seamus Heaney and *Maggot* by Paul Muldoon are both shortlisted for the *Irish Times* Poetry Now Award. ¶ *Night* by David Harsent is shortlisted for the Forward Prize for Best Collection. ¶ 'Bees' by Jo Shapcott is shortlisted for the Forward Prize for Best Single Poem. ¶ A new digital edition of T. S. Eliot's *The Waste Land* for iPad is launched, bringing to life one of the most revolutionary poems of the last hundred years, illuminated by a wealth of interactive features. ¶ The Queen's Gold Medal for Poetry is awarded to Jo Shapcott. ¶ At Westminster Abbey a memorial is dedicated to Ted Hughes in Poets' Corner. ¶

2012 *The Death of King Arthur* by Simon Armitage is shortlisted for the T. S. Eliot Prize. ¶ *The World's Two Smallest Humans* by Julia Copus is shortlisted for the T. S. Eliot Prize and the Costa Poetry Award. ¶ David Harsent's collection *Night* wins the 2012 International Griffin Poetry Prize. ¶ *81 Austerities* by Sam Riviere wins the Felix Dennis Prize for Best First Collection, one of the Forward Prizes for Poetry. ¶ *Farmers Cross* by Bernard O'Donoghue is shortlisted for the *Irish Times* Poetry Now Award. ¶

2013 The Forward Prize for Best First Collection is awarded to Emily Berry for *Dear Boy.* ¶ Hugo Williams is shortlisted for the Forward Prize for Best Single

Poem for 'From the Dialysis Ward'. ¶ Alice Oswald is awarded the Warwick Prize for Writing for her collection *Memorial*, which also wins the Poetry Society's Corneliu M. Popescu Prize for poetry in translation. ¶ The Queen's Gold Medal for Poetry is awarded to Douglas Dunn. ¶ The shortlist for the 2013 T. S. Eliot Prize includes Daljit Nagra for *The Ramayana: A Retelling* and Maurice Riordan for *The Water Stealer*. ¶ *Pink Mist* by Owen Sheers wins the Hay Festival Medal for Poetry. ¶ In his eulogy for Seamus Heaney, Paul Muldoon says, 'We remember the beauty of Seamus Heaney – as a bard, and in his being.' In November the first official tribute evenings to Heaney are held at Harvard, then in New York, followed by events at the Royal Festival Hall in London, the Waterfront Hall, Belfast, and the Sheldonian, Oxford. ¶

2014 Maurice Riordan is shortlisted for the Pigott Poetry Prize for *The Water Stealer*. ¶ Hugo Williams is shortlisted for the Forward Prize for Best Collection for *I Knew the Bride*. ¶ Daljit Nagra is awarded the Society of Authors Travelling Scholarship. ¶ Nick Laird's *Go Giants* is shortlisted for the *Irish Times* Poetry Now Award. ¶ Emily Berry, Emma Jones and Daljit Nagra are announced as three of the Poetry Book Society's Next Generation Poets 2014. ¶ *Pink Mist* by Owen Sheers is named the Wales Book of the Year after winning the poetry category. ¶

2015 *Fire Songs* by David Harsent is awarded the T. S. Eliot Prize for Poetry. ¶ Alice Oswald wins the Ted Hughes Award for New Work for *Tithonus*, a poem and performance commissioned by London's Southbank Centre. ¶ *One Thousand Things Worth Knowing* by Paul Muldoon wins the Pigott Poetry Prize. ¶ Don Paterson is awarded the Neustadt International Prize for Literature. ¶ *Terror* by Toby Martinez de las Rivas is shortlisted for the Seamus Heaney Centre for Poetry's Prize for First Full Collection. ¶ Paul Muldoon's *One Thousand Things Worth Knowing* is shortlisted for the Forward Prize for Best Collection. ¶ James Fenton is awarded the Pen Pinter Prize. ¶ *40 Sonnets* by Don Paterson wins the Costa Poetry Award, and is shortlisted for the T. S. Eliot Prize.

Acknowledgements

Poetry

All poetry reprinted by permission of Faber & Faber unless otherwise stated.

'Paper Aeroplane' taken from *Paper Aeroplane* © Simon Armitage

'Another Unfortunate Choice' taken from *Two Cures for Love, Selected Poems 1979–2006* © Wendy Cope

'La Figlia Che Piange' taken from *The Poems Volume One* © Estate of T. S. Eliot

'Kata' taken from *The Casual Perfect* © Lavinia Greenlaw

'The Underground' taken from *New Selected Poems 1966–1987* © Estate of Seamus Heaney. Reprinted by permission of Farrar, Straus & Giroux, LLC., New York

'The day he died' taken from *Collected Poems* © Estate of Ted Hughes. Reprinted by permission of Farrar, Straus & Giroux, LLC., New York

'Sonnet' taken from *The Striped World* © Emma Jones

'Friday Night in the Royal Station Hotel' taken from *The Complete Poems* © Estate of Philip Larkin. Reprinted by permission of Farrar, Straus & Giroux, LLC., New York

'Blackdown Song' taken from *Terror* © Toby Martinez de las Rivas

'A Jelly-Fish' taken from *The Poems of Marianne Moore* © Estate of Marianne Moore. Reprinted by permission of Penguin Publishing Group, New York

'The Conclusion of Joseph Turrill' taken from *Peace Talks* © Andrew Motion. Reprinted by permission of WME

'A Porcupine' taken from *Maggot* © Paul Muldoon. Reprinted by permission of Farrar, Straus & Giroux, New York

'Rama's second take . . . He as Vishnu and she as Lakshmi' taken from *Ramayana: A Retelling* © Daljit Nagra

'The Roundabout' taken from *40 Sonnets* © Don Paterson

'Shy Willows' taken from *Love's Bonfire* © Tom Paulin

'Crossing the Water' taken from *Crossing the Water* © Estate of Sylvia Plath. Reprinted by permission of HarperCollins Publishers, New York

'Last of the Campus Poems' taken from *Nonsense* © Christopher Reid. Reprinted by permission of the author, c/o Rogers, Coleridge & White Ltd., 20 Powis Mews, London W11 1JN

Picture Credits

All jacket designs by Berthold Wolpe except for:

Old Possum's Book of Practical Cats, illustrations by T. S. Eliot
Death of a Naturalist, design by Faber
The Waste Land, design by Faber
Sylvia Plath Poems Chosen by Carol Ann Duffy, design by Faber, painting by Sylvia Plath © Estate of
    Sylvia Plath
Reading Chaucer's Poems, design by Faber, illustration by Eleanor Crow
Making Cocoa for Kingsley Amis, design by Pentagram
The Collected Poems & Drawings of Stevie Smith, design by Faber, drawing by Stevie Smith © The Stevie
    Smith Papers, 1976.012. Special Collections, McFarlin Library, The University of Tulsa
The Dying Gaul, design by David Jones © Estate of David Jones
The New Faber Book of Love Poems, design by Faber

NOTES

NOTES

Faber Members is a free-to-join membership programme that brings readers closer to Faber and to the books and authors that they love.

Sign up now for exclusive access to literary events, discounts on Faber books and to our range of beautiful hand-bound Collectors' Editions.

Become a Faber Member today at fabermembers.com

FABER ACADEMY
—*creative writing courses with character*—

faceracademy.co.uk/**courses**

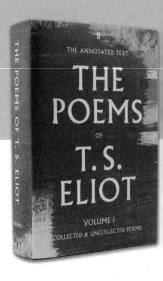

Eiléan Ní
Chuilleanáin
Selected
Poems

Amy
Clampitt
Collected
Poems

Douglas
Dunn
New
Selected
Poems
1964–1999

Lawrenc
Durrell
Selected
Poems
Edited by Peter Porter

Robert
Henryson
The Testament
of Cresseid &
Seven Fables
Translated by
Seamus
Heaney

Michael
Hofmann
Selected
Poems

Mick
Imlah
Selected
Poems

August
Kleinzahl
Sleeping I
Off in
Rapid Cit
New and Selected Poem

Jamie
McKendrick
Crocodiles
& Obelisks

Jamie
McKendrick
Ink Stone

Dorothy
Molloy
Gethsemane
Day

Doroth
Molloy
Hare
Soup

Tom Paulin
The Road
to Inver

Maurice
Riordan
The Holy
Land

Frederick
Seidel
Selected
Poems

Charles
Simic
Selected
Poems
1963–2003